THE TRUTH ABOUT MARRIAGE LICENSE LAWS

INTRODUCTION

The reason I am writing about this subject, marriage license is because in my last marriage I ask God were there any way I could get married without a marriage license, this was my question to the Most High. So as I was researching on the computer, what I found in the Black's Law Dictionary is why we shouldn't get married with State Marriage License. I couldn't believe what I had found, this is why I always say if you want to know something, make sure you are ready for the answer from the Most High. I always believe in the law of man and had not read about it because no one was talking about it, this is why following man and not wanting to know the truth will leave us ignorant. Wisdom and knowledge don't come overnight. We wonder why our marriages don't last, sometime we

enter it for the wrong reason and it is not love it can be lust, sex and money. Putting the Government in our affairs they have taken over instead of helping, they are all about making money instead of keeping family's together. Divorces, Children taken away and men's especially our black men's. This is a way to keep our Brothers, husbands down where they feel they can't get up. All our men need to take their power back. Our men are somebody and always will be. Our Black men have power if only they knew it and use it by coming together with each other. Together we stand, divide we fall. It's hard to break us when we stand together. If we separate we lose our power and we can easily be broken as a black nation. Some of us have guns, however we are using it in the wrong way to kill each other. What we are doing for the black nation is depopulating

our nation. Open your eyes, need I say anymore. We need to pray about the right way to be join together as husband and wives. The Government got rid of Common Law Marriages because the judges and lawyers seen how they could make money from us, this is my opinion. I am writing to open our spiritual eyes and mind to what is happening around us and this have not just started , this been going on a while. Let's not be blind anymore concerning marriage license. I will be writing some scripture concening what it say about marrige. I don't know a lot about all marriages, I only know about my own. We have to be careful what we say in our vows, because our words carry power. This is a protestant vow, maybe some of us have quoted when we had gotten married. This is just an example of one:
I ____________, take thee ______________, to be

my wedded wife/ husband, to have and to hold from this day forward, for better, for worse (Leave Out), in sickness (Leave out) and in health, to love and to cherish, till death (leave Out), do us part, according to God's holy ordinance; and there to I pledge thee my faith. This my opinion, with the words I said leave out, which mean you have already curse your marriage. The one I do like is ___________, I now take you to be my wedded wife/ husband, to live together after God's ordinance in the Holy relationship of marriage. I promise to love and comfort you, honor and keep you, and forsaking all others, I will be yours alone as long as we both shall live. You can say any vows you and your partner agree on. However when I ever get married again I don't want to get a marriage license. As I close I will go into more detail on what God say (Our Higher Power) and what the Black's Law Dictionary also say. We are destroyed for a lack of knowledge : Hosea 4:6, because thou hast rejected knowledge,I will also reject thee that thou shalt be no priest to me: seeing thou hast forgotten the law of thy God, I will also forget thy children. So enjoy this information that I am going to impart in our mind, wisdom, knowledge and understanding the best I can. I send peace, love and blessings to everyone who take time to read or buy this book for yourself or someone else.

Love Always Author: Wanda Chellers

CONTENT

CHAPTER 1

WHAT IS A CONSTITUTES MARRIAGE?

Though one may be over powered two can defend themselves. A cord of three strands is not quickly broken."
Ecclesiastes 4:12

A constitutes marriage in the Bible it simply consists of a man and woman, with the consent of the woman's father or guardian, living together and attempting procreation. No vows, no pirest, no ritual, no prayer, no pronouncement, no license, no registration. This is quite different from how we define and enact marriage today. In other word for a marriage to be real today it must be legal, which must be recognized by laws of the State. For many Christians, a marriage is not a Christian marriage unless it is officiated by a minister that work with the state which makes a verbal pronouncement in the presence of a congregation. For in human history, marriage has been an agreement, recognized or arranged by immediate families, for a man and woman to live together. Marriage as a legal institution and a religious ceremony, began as a result of the reformation. In the middle age Churches kept records of who was married to whom. Luther viewed marriages as a worldly matter, so he turned over the recording of marriages to the State. Calvin believed for a marriage to be valid it needed to be both recorded by State and Officiated by the Church. In European they had three kind of marriages which were legal, religious and social. Social Marriage is the most biblical. The social benefits of marriage: It is a positively out come which includes improved cognitive, emotional and physical well-being for children, bettermental and physical health for adults, and greater earnings and consumption for family members. Married couples have better physical health, more financial stability, and greater social mobility than sometime unmarried people. We are the building blocks of civilization. This is a puzzle marriage ceremonies missing in the Bible. There are people who was married in the Bible, I have not found no description of any ceremonies in it. Adam and Eve made for each other, they were married with the procreate. Jacob married Leah by mistake, it was he consummated the marriage in the darkness of a tent.

Jesus attended a wedding in Cana which was a family party, however there was no ceremony that was described. There is a ceremony in the Bible in Tobit 7: 12-14 which the father places the hand of his daughter in the hand of her husband, then he writes a contract. There are no ceremony in the Bible because marriages didn't involve a cermony . Marriage in the Bible consists of a man and woman, with the consent of the woman father or guardian, living together and attempting procreation, which I have wrote in this same chapter. In the beginning no vows, no priest, no ritual, no prayer, no pronouncement,

no license, no registration.
Scriptures for constitute a marriage.
For the Man: It is promise to love his
wife as Christ love the Church
(Ephesians 5:25).
It is to leave his parents and cleave
alone to his wife. (Ephesians 5: 31).
It is a promise of monogamy (1
Corinthians 7, Hebrews 13: 4).

For the Woman: It is a promise of
Monogamy (1 Corinthians 7, Hebrew
13: 4).
It is a promise to joyfully submit to
her husband. (Ephesians 5: 22).
It is a promise to respect her
husband.

Therefore, for a marriage to be a marriage in the eye of God, a covenant must be part of the process.

CHAPTER 2

MARRIAGE LICENSING SCRIPTURES

Wealth is not his that has it, but his who enjoys it.
Benjamin Franklin

Hebrews 13:4
Genesis 2:24
1 Peter 3:7
Matthew 19:5
Matthew 5:31
Ephesians 5:25
Mark 10:12
Proverbs 18:22
1 Corinthians 6:16
Matthew 5:32

Romans 7:2

1 John 1:9

Colossians 3:18-19

1 Corinthians 7:1-40

Matthew 19:4-6

Proverbs 31:10

Exodus 22:16

Genesis 2:18

Ephesians 5:31

1 Corinthians 7:2

Mark 10:9

Deuteronomy 24:5

Genesis 16:9

Matthew 9:19

Malachi 2:14

Exodus 20:14

1 Peter 4:8

Ephesians 5:-22-23

1 Corinthians 7:3

1 Corinthians 6:11

1 Corinthians 6:9

Matthew 19:12

Matthew 19:6

Matthew 5:1-48

Numbers 4:1-49

Leviticus 18:22

Exodus 22:16-17

Genesis 2:22-24

Genesis 2:1-25

Genesis 1:27

Ephesians 5:33

Ephesians 5:32

Ephesians 5:28

Ephesians 5:22-33

Ephesians 4:32

2 Corinthians 6:14

1 Corinthians 7:3-4

Romans 1:27

John 4:16-18

Mark 12:25

Matthew 22:30

Malachi 2:14-15

Isaiah 54:5

Proverbs 19:14

Proverbs 16:9

Genesis 24:67

Genesis 1:28

Genesis 1:27-28

1 Timothy 5:14

1 Timothy 3:3

Colossians 3:19

Ephesians 5:25-26

Ephesians 5:25-33

Ephesians 4:2-3

1 Corinthians 13:4-7

1 Corinthians 7:3-5

Mark 10:6-9

Ecclesiastes 4:9-12

Proverbs 12:4

Deuteronomy 24:1-4

1 John 4:18

1 Timothy 5:8

Ephesians 5:22-24

Ephesians 5:21

1 Corinthians 16:14

1 Corinthians 13:13

CHAPTER 3

MARRIAGE LICENSES OR CONTRACTS , DID IT EXIST IN BIBLE TIMES?

All that we are is a result of what we have thought.
Buddha

In the past there are no biblical history where people were married by a contract of the law. This started in the United States. We can look at Adam and Eve and they didn't have a church wedding nor sign a marriage contract, it was God will for them to be married since he created them. They were the first couple on the planet. (Genesis 2:18-25). Look at Cain and Mary in Genesis 4:17, Genesis 24 it talk about Isaac and Rebekah marry. Genesis 29:18, Both marriages are examples of marriage by agreement and may have included a formal document, the scripture didn't say this occurred. Wife by covenant is in Malachi 2:14. My opinion is when a man and woman come together as husband and wife this is a commitment, all is needed between two people is for them to consider the relationship is valid and lawful. This is a covenant between a man and woman concerning their continuing relationship A marriage relationship using private contract is not sinful based on God word. It should be witnessed by two parties, so it can not be deny that the wedding occurred. (Deuteronomy 17: 6). People can do their own marriage contract, I feel this is the best way to keep the government out of your business. There are different types of contracts. Georgia Code 19-3-63 (2020)- construction of marriage contract. Such marriage contract shall be in writing, signed by both parties who agree to be bound, and attested by at least two witnesses, one of whom shall be a notary public. There are two marriage contracts: Community of property or an ante nuptial agreement. If you choose to be married in community of property, your assets are shared equally. If not, you need to sign an ante nuptial agreement before you get married. So let's break it down about a marriage contract in an agreement signed before or after a wedding that provides a private and custom-made set of rules for dividing the couple's property should they separate and divorce or pass away. In fact a marriage contract can over lap in many of its functions with a will. These are the three types of marital agreements:

Prenuptial (or ante-nuptial) agreement, Post-nuptial agreement, Separation agreement. In your spare time take time to do a research on these. Now we have some kind of understanding on a marital contract. Now let's get some understanding about Marriage License: A marriage license is a document issued, either by a Religious Organization or State Authority, authorizing a couple to get married. A married license is what you get first, which is basically an application to be married. After you fill it out, had a ceremony, gotten it signed, the officiant has turn it back into the county, then you receive a marriage certificate. This will prove that a person is officially married by man law. Say if you want to get married this way, there are step by step instruction how how to. There is a fee that will typically run you between $35.00 and $150.00 depending on your State and County. So now we know the different between license and contract. Just remember I am still learning at my age. I am season just right.

CHAPTER 4

MARRIED LAWS BY STATES

Happiness is not in the mere possession of money; it lies in the joy of achievement, in the thrill of creative effort.

1. Alabama: In Alabama there is not a waiting period, however your marriage licenses are only valid for thirity days. Legal age is nine-teen years old and identification. If you are a resident you don't have to wait to get married. In some counties none residents are required to wait three days before a ceremony.

If you are under age you have to be 16 with parental or legal guardian consent and eighteen with out parental or legal guardian consent. Your license will expire 30 days after it is issued. There is waiting time to receive when you apply for a marriage license. Blood Test: No, Proxy Marriages Legal: No, Witnesses Needed: No.

2. Alaska: You don't have to be a state resident to get an Alaska marrage license. If you are hosting an Alaska wedding you need to arrive a few days early because there is a three day waiting period between receiving your marrage

license and when you can wed. You need identification. You must be 18 years old. The license will expire in three months. You will have to wait three days (business days) before receiving your marriage license. No Blood Test, No Proxy Marriages Legal, Witnesses Yes, it have to be two witnesses present at the ceremony.

3. Arizona: There is no waiting period to receive your marriage license and wedding, the license are valid for 12 months. You will need Identification, state resident is not required to get a marriage license. You must be at age 18

and if you are under age 18, court and parental/ guardian consent is required. The license will be valid up to 12 months. No waiting time. No Blood Test, No Proxy Marriages Legal, Need two witnesses and the officiant must sign the marriage license at the ceremony.

4. Arkansas: There is no waiting period for couples over 18, the marriage licenses are valid for 60 days. Identification is needed, state resident is not required, a marriage license from Arkansas can be used any where in the State. If you are under age, parental consent is required with a five day wait period.

Both parties must be 18 year old to get married without parental consent. Marriage license is valid for 60 days. There is not wait if both parties are over 18. No blood test is required, not witnesses.

5. California: Most place in California is priciest places like Los Angeles and San Francisco, but more rural spots in the state can be more affordable. You must have a valid ID., you don't need to be a resident of California to get a marriage license. Age both parties should be over 18, to married without parental consent. Married license expire 90 days after issued,

you will receive the license the same day you submit the application. No blood test is required. Proxy Marriages Legal, No, Witnesses, a California marriage license requires the signature of one witness but a space up to two.

6. Colorado: You don't have to be a resident of the state to receive a marriage license in Colorado. Each partner need a ID, age have to be 18 or older, if you are between 16 and 17 both parties must have parental consent form and must be notarized and anyone under 15, a court order is required. The license is valid

for 35 days and must be returned for recording with in 63 days. No wait time, no blood test, proxy marriage legal: yes, but only if one party is unable to be present due to illness or they are out of the state. Witnesses no.

7. Connecticut: Identification is needed, you should know your officiant's name, phone number, and address along with the ceremony location. You don't need to be a resident to receive a marriage license, but you need to apply either in the town where the applicant lives or the town where you plan on getting married. Age both should be

18 or older, the married license expire in 65 days. Wait time none, blood test none, proxy marriage legal : no, witnesses not required.

8. Delaware: You will need photo ID., dont need to be a state resident, age 18 or older, license expire in 30 days, waiting time is 24 hours period from the time of application. No blood test, no proxy marriages, witnesses: Two witnesses, at least 18 years of age at the time of the ceremony.

9. District Of Columbia: ID. Is required, there is no residency requirement, age you must be 18

years of age to be married in DC without parental consent. When license is issued your license don't expire. Waiting time there is none. No blood test, proxy marriages legal: yes, a third party can apply on the couple's behalf and have to have proper ID for the couple as well as the fee, No witnesses.

10. Florida: Valid ID photo, you may be asked for a certified copy of your birth certificate. You don't have to be a state resident. Age must be 18 years of age or older to be married without parental consent. No one under 16 can be married in Florida. Married license is valid for 60 days

after issued. Wait time is 3 days for Florida residents who have not completed premarital course, no wait for non-Florida residents. Blood test no, proxy marriages legal: no, Witnesses no.

11. Georgia: Need a valid form photo ID, when submitting a marriage license application. No resident requirement, however none-residents have to apply in the county where your marriage is being preformed. Age must be 18 or older. If any one is under age 25, the clerk may require a proof of age. No one under the age of 16 will be issued a marriage license.

License will not expire once it has been issued. No wait period, no blood test, proxy marriage legal, no, Witnesses none.

12. Hawaii: Valid ID and proof of age is required. Don't have to be a resident to receive a marriage license. Age is 18 year of age, the minimum age is 15 with written consent from parent/ guardian as well as written approval from a judge in family court. The license is valid for 30 days on any Islands. No waiting period, no blood test, proxy marriage legal, no witnesses None.

13. Idaho: Both person must have an ID.

as well as an original birth certificate or certified copy. State resident not required. Age must be 18 for both person or older, 16 to 17 must be accompanied by parent or legal guardian. Anyone under 16 must obtain permission from the court. No expired day after license have been issued . No wait time, no blood test, proxy marriage legal no, witnesses no.

14. Illinois: ID an up to date photo is required. You don't have to be a resident of Illinois to get a married license. Age both must be 18, between the age of 16-18,

parental consent is required. No one under age 16 can married in Illinois. License is valid for 60 days when issued. There a 24 hour wait period between submitting the application and receiving your marriage certificate. No blood test, no proxy marriage legal, witnesses none.

15. Indiana: If you're from out of town, you must apply for a marriage license in the town where your wedding is taking place. ID have to be current. State resident is not required. Legal age is 18 years old. If 17 you must have both parents/ guardians present to sign consent.

Under 17 both parties must go through a court process. License will expire 60 days after it has been issued. No wait time, no blood test, no proxy marriage legal, witnesses none.

16. Iowa: Iowa wedding is ideal for couples who want a more pastoral setting. Both person need Photo ID. No state resident is required. You have to be 18. People between 16-17 can only get married with special permission from a judge and one parental/ guardian must be present. No expiration date unless it isn't picked up within six months from the date of application . Wait period

of 3 business days before license is valid and the actual marriage can occur. Blood test no, Proxy no, however if one person can't be present, they can sign the license application before a notary public at a different location. Witness: one witness over age 18 is required.

17. Kansas: A ID and social security card required. You don't have to be a resident. You must be 18 years old, the minimum age to get married is 15, must have parent/ guardian consent and consent from a judge. License will expire 6 months after the issue date. Wait time is 3 business days. No blood test,

proxy no, witnesses, witness yes, witnesses are needed and must be over 18 years of age.

18. Kentucky: Both parties must have photo ID, original birth certificate and social security card. Don't have to be a resident. Legal age is 18. If under 18, must have parental consent and be issued in the county where the couple lives. License will expire 30 days after it has been issued. There is no wait time. No blood test, proxy no, witnesses yes, need two witnesses other than the couple, must be present.

19. Louisiana: ID is required, you don't have to be a resident. Legal age 18. The minimum age is 16 and both parents mus be present at time of the application. License will expire 30 days after issued. Wait time is 72 hour period between the time the license is issued and the ceremony. No blood test, proxy no, witnesses yes, need two are required to sign the license at the ceremony.

20. Maine: ID both partners, you don't need to be a resident. Age require is 18, anyone under age of 18 must have parental consent and anyone 16 years old must notify a judge.

License expire after 90 days. There is no wait time, blood test no, proxy no, witnesses needed: must be witness by two people other than the officiant.

21. Maryland: ID is required and know your social security number. No state resident is required. Legal age is 18, and between the age of 15-17 you can't get married without parental/ guardian consent and proof the female is pregnant or has given birth to a child. The license will expire in 6 months. The wait period is 48 hours. No blood test, proxy no, witnesses no.

22. Massachusetts: Photo ID, and social security numbers. You don't have to be a resident, however you must have a valid Massachusetts marriage license. The legal age is 18 or older, minor must fill out an application with the court. License is valid 60 days once it is issued. There is a mandatory waiting period for 3 days, not including the day of the application. No blood test, Proxy no, unless one of the partner's is in military or incarcerated. Intentions can be filed by either party as long as one of them is a resident of Massachusetts. No witnesses.

23. Michigan: Both must have valid photo ID, current address, birth ceretificate/ social security number, valid passport. Residents must file their application in the county where they reside. None-residents must file their application in the county where they are going to be married. Legal age is 18. If you're 16 or 17, they can get married with parental consent. If 15 or younger, court approval is also needed. License is valid for 33 days. There is a three days wait period between application submission and the license is issued. No blood test, proxy no, but only one of the partners need to be present and have all the required paper work along with a copy of the other person's photo ID. Witnesses yes, You will need two witnesses to sign the marriage license.

24. Minnesota: ID with photo. You don't have to be a resident, legal age is 18, under this age you have to ge parental consent or court approval. License is valid for 6 months. No wait period, no blood test, proxy no: however, if only one of the partners is available, the other must fill out a supplemental form and have it notarized. Witnesses: Must be two witnesses adult 16 years of age or older.

25. Mississippi: Must have a valid ID both person. You don't have to be a resident. Legal age is 21, anyone under the age of 21, parental consent is needed. A license will not be issued unless the male is at least 17 and the female is at least 15. License has no expiration date. No wait time license effective immediately. No blood test, proxy no, witnesses none.

26. Missouri : ID with photo and proff of age for all parties. You don't need to be resident. Legal age is 19 or older with valid ID along with social security card. Under the age of 19 both need their birth

certificate as well. If you are between 16-17 parental consent must be given. Marriage license will not be given if one person is 21 and the other is under 18. License is valid for 30 days, there is no wait time. Blood test no, proxy: yes, witnesses no.

27. Montana : ID and proof of age. None residents have to otain a license in the county where they are getting married. Legal age is 18, if you are under this age you have to get parental consent, along with two counseling sessions, and court approval. License will expire 180 days. No wait time, blood test :

Women under the age of 50 are required to take a Rubella blood test unless they request to waive it. Proxy- yes, witnesses – none.

28. Nebraska: Need ID and proof of age. Don't need to be a resident. Legal age is 19 years old, if under age 19, a notarized consent form must be signed by both parents/ guardians. No one under 17 can be married in Nebraska. License is valid for one year from date issued. No waiting period, no blood test required. Proxy- no, witnesses- yes: two witnesses are required to be present at the ceremony.

29. Nevada : Need ID from both person. You don't need to be resident, legal age is 18 years old, if you are between 16-17 one legal guardian/ parent must be present, under 16 required a court order. License is valid for one year. No waiting time, no blood test, proxy no, witnesses none.

30. New Hampshire: ID and proof of age is required. No resident is required. The minimum age is 16. License will expire 90 days from the filing of application. No wait period, however it is not valid for the first 3 days after it has been issued. No blood test, proxy no, witnesses no.

31. New Jersey : ID is needed, your social security card/ number. Don't need to be a resident. Legal age is 18 years old. License valid for 6 months. There is a 72 hour wait period. No blood test, proxy no, witnesses- You will need a witness, who is over 18, present when applying for a marriage license.

32. New Mexico: Need a photo ID. You don't have to be a resident. Legal age is 18 years old. No expiration, however it have to be returned 90 days after the ceremony. No wait time., no blood test, no proxy, witnesses none.

33. New York: Both need ID. Don't need to be a resident. Legal age 18 without a parental consent. License is valid for 60 days or 180 days for active military personnel. There is a 24- hour wait period before the wedding ceremony can be formed. No blood test, proxy no, witnesses: one person must witness your signature, be at least 18 years old.

34. North Carolina: Both parties need ID, social security card or tax form with number and name. Don't need to be a resident. Legal age is 18 without parental consent. License will expire in 60 days. There is no wait period. No Blood test, no proxty, witnesses: two witnesses are required at all ceremonies.

35. North Dakota: ID photo needed. Don't need to be a resident, legal age is 18 with parental consent. License is valid for 30 days. No blood test, proxy no, witnesses: two witnesses must be present when application filed out.

36. Ohio- ID, and know your social security number. If you are a resident you must apply in the county where you live. If none-resident you must apply where the ceremony is taking place.

Legal age is 18 without parental consent. License is valid for 60 days. No wait period, no blood test, proxy no, witnesses none.

37. Oklahoma: Both person have to have birth certificate translated in english. Don't have to be a resident and license can be use state wide. Legal age is 18 years old with parental consent. License is vlid for 10 days. There is no wait time if you are over 18 years old. If under 18, there is a 72 hour waiting period. No blood test, proxy no, witnesses: two witnesses signatures are required.

38. Oregon: Both need ID valid.

Don't need to be resident. Legal age is 18, without parental consent, no one under the age of 17 can be married in Oregan. License is valid for 60 days. There is a waiting period of 3 days. No blood test, proxy none, witnesses: two witnesses, at least 18 years old.

39. Pennsylvania: Both need ID and social security card. Don't have to be a resident. Legal age is 18, without parental consent. License valid for 60 days once issued. There are 3 days wait period between applying and receiving the license. No blood test, proxy no, witnesses no.

40. Rhode Island: ID and birth certificates needed. Resident must apply in the city/ town where they live. None- resident must apply where wedding will be taking place. Legal age is 18, without parental consent. License is valid for 90 days. No wait period, blood test no, proxy no, witnesses- two witnesses, over 18, must be present at the ceremony.

41. South Carolina: A valid photo ID for both parties and social security number. You don't have to be a resident. Legal age both need to be 18, without parental consent. License will not expire. There are

a 24 hours wait period after application is made before the license can be picked up by the couple. No blood test, proxy no, no witnesses.

42. South Dakota: Both partners must have photo ID. You don't have to be a resident. Legal age is 18, without parental consent. License is valid for 20 days. No wait period, no blood test, no proxy, no witnesses.

43. Tennessee: Need Photo ID, as well as your social security number. Don't need to be a resident. Legal age 18 without parental consent.

License is valid for 30 days. No wait period, no blood test, proxy no, unless an individual is incarcerated or has a disability, which prevents them from appearing. In this case, a notarized statement is required with the person's name, age, and current address along with their next of kin's information, witnesses no.

44. Texas: Valid photo ID. Don't need to be a resident. Legal age is 18 without parental concent. License is valid for 90 days. Wait time is 72 hours waiting period, unless you are active military. No blood test, proxy Yes, but only for active military members who are

stationed outside of the country, witnesses none.

45. Utah: Valid photo ID and social security number. Don't need to be a resident. Legal age is 18, without parental consent. License valid for 30 days. No wait period, no blood test, proxy no, witnesses: two witnesses over age 18 must be present at ceremony.

46. Vermont: Both need a valid ID. Resident must get their license in the city/ town where they reside. None- residents, get their from any where in the state. Legal age 18, without parental consent. License

valid for 60 days. No wait time, blood test no, no proxy, no witnesses.

47. Virginia: Both need photo ID. Don't need to be a resident. Legal age 18, without parental consent. License will expire in 60 days. No wait time, no blood test, no proxy, no witnesses.

48. Washington: Need photo ID with birth date. You don't have to be a resident. Legal age is 18, without parental consent. License is valid for 60 days. There is a three day wait period, no blood test, no proxy, unless you both unable to apply at the same time, one person may fill out an absentee form. Witnesses: two witnesses must be present at the time of the ceremony.

49. West Virginia: Both need a valid photo ID or certified copy of their birth certificate, social security numbers, and their parents names. If you are a resident apply in the state where you reside, if not you can apply anywhere state wide. Legal age is 18. Your license is valid for 60 days. No wait period if couple is over 18 years old, if partners are under 18, there is a 72 hour wait period. No blood test, no proxy, no witnesses.

50. Wisconsin: Photo ID is required. Resident must apply in the county where they reside, none- residents must apply in the county where they plan to be married. Legal age is 18. License is valid for 30 days. Wait period is 5 days unless it is waived for an additional cost. No blood test, no proxy, need two witnesses adults must be present at the time of the ceremony.

51. Wyoming: Both need photo ID. Don't need to be a resident. Legal age is 18, without parental consent. Licenses is valid for one year. No wait time, no blood test, no proxy, witnesses: two witnesses are required to be at the ceremony.

CHAPTER 5

WHAT IS A COMMITMENT CEREMONY?

Empty pockets never held anyone back. Only empty heads and empty hearts can do that.

A commitment ceremony is a marriage ceremony in which two people commit their lives to each other, but it isn't legally binding. Commitment ceremonies can look like a legally binding wedding, however a couple doesn't go off to sign paper work to make it legal by the government standards. There are other names for commitment ceremonies which are spiritual symbolic or promise ceremonies. Commitment ceremonies is just as valid and important to relationship as having a civil (government) backing. So people choose to do legal ceremony or paper work before or after their commitment ceremony, however the choice would be yours. Why people choose to have a commitment ceremony? 1. Couple who can't get married by law, same sex marriage because at first the United States didn't accept these type marriages nationwide. Same sex marriage is still illegal in parts of the world. Many couples choose a commitment ceremony as the relationship is not legally recognized. Commitment ceremonies allow these groups to celebrate their love and relationship, without government approval. Couples who do want to be legally married.

2. Couples who don't want to be legally married, this happen because it's personal, which they might be financially disadvantaged as a marriage couple, it might be due to taxes, disability benefits or

other needs. Some people are not religious, and marriage defined by the state don't appel to some people, however they want to commit to each other: this is also the couples want the state out of their ceremony without ever having to answer to the government on the status of the relationship.

3. Couple inconvenience in getting legally married. Some people want to have their marriage in different country or state. If you get married in a country that you are not a citizen it might take months to get a notarized copy of your marriage certificate. Some place might

require blood tests, wait periods or ask for you to arrive weeks in advance and apply for your license in person. Pros of commitment ceremonies: You can get married when and wherever you want. If your state has a waiting period, let it go by saying your vows, commit your lives together, and sign the papers whenever it is convenient for you. If you do your commitment ceremony and paper work another day, you can get married any where in the world you want. In commitment ceremonies there are no script, you may say exactly what you want in your vows, you can have officiate. You can have your mom, friend or dog to be the person standing with you and your partner during your ceremony. The cons in commitment ceremonies. If you decide to have commitment ceremony and then go the legal way on a different date, then this will results in two anniversaries. You can ditch the legal date and use the ceremony date. Just remember when you are filing out official paper work in the future you need to remember the date of the government that you got married. Until legally married you can't claim benefits. You will have to check single on your offical documents, it will be hard to change your name

if you don't have a marriage
certificates as a supporting
document. Some old-fashioned
family sometime will not approve.
People who love you should support
your decisions. Sometime religion or
personal experience might be a
reason some feel uneasy, seeing a
commitment ceremony as real
marriage. Please don't discourage,
just be happy. You might want to get
started with these questions:

1. Where do I want to get married?
2. What activites to do on our
wedding day?
3. Do I want an officiant who will
perform a non-legal ceremony

or self solemnize?

4. Do I want to invite guests or do I want it to be two witnesses or just be the two of us?

You can write personal vows or find other ways to let love ones into your day even when they are not physically present. Commitment ceremonies is just for couples who want to get married their own way. You can get married your way because you are the master of your own ship. After your commitment ceremony then you can get married by the law of man or whatever is best for you both, this is why communication in a relationship is

72

important. Without communication and understanding, there is not a relationship. This mean you'll are not on the same page and it can cause a situation in a relationship. Wisdom is the principle thing therefore, get wisdom and all thy getting, get an understanding. (Proverbs 4:7)

CHAPTER 6

WHAT IS COMMON LAW MARRIAGE?

Gratitude is the vital ingredient in the recipe for faith.
Magus Incognito

A common law marriage is a marriage that is established without legal formalities like getting a marriage license or having a religious or civil ceremony. The features of a common law marrriage are, two people come together as a marriage couple. They live together, and in the publicly they are seen a married couple. When they come together as a common law couple, they will live in a state that recognizes common law marriage. They will meet the basic requirement under state law for a legal common law marriage, then there marriage is like any other marriage. They will enjoy all rights and benefits which are: Inheritance rights and other

74

estate planning benefits, social security benefits, tax treatment, employment benefits and to ask the court to divide your property and award alimony when ending a marriage. Over the year most state in the United States have stopped allowing these informal marriages, through either their laws or court dicisions (known as case law). when living in the right place, you have to meet the requirements under the marriage law in your state, such as: Being old enough to get married (usually 18 years old). Having mental capacity to enter into a marriage. Not being close related to your spouse, and not being married to anyone else. Both partner have to establish a common law marriage with all of the legal and social responsibilites of marriage. How can you prove someone state of mind without a marriage license or ceremony? This might be easy if the couple signed an agreement or other written document. In Texas allow couples to register their informal marriage by filing a declaration with the county clerk. (tex. Fam. Code 2.401,2.402 (2022). This is a conduct that demonstrate your intention to be in a common law marriage which is: presenting yourselves to family, friends and your community as a married couple.

Using words saying husband, wife or spouse when referring to each other, as well in documents like a loan applications, leases and insurance forms. Open joint bank accounts. Sharing your income, property and expenses. Filing joint tax returns and wearing wedding rings. The question is how long do you have to live together to be in a common law marriage? The myth is 7 years is just that which is just a myth. None of the States that recognize these marriages have set a minimum amount of time that you should live together before your relationship qualifies. So let go back to which States recognize common law marriages: Only Nine

States in the United States (Plus Washington, D.C.) allow couples to establish new common law marriages. These are the current recognize valid common law marriage states regardless when it were established, either in state laws or as a result of court rulings:

1. Colorado (Colo. Rev. Stat. 14-2109.5)
2. District Of Columbia (case law)
3. Iowa (Iowa Code 252A.3.6.595.1A)
4. Kansas (kan. Stat. 23-2502,23-2714 (b))
5. Montana (Mont. Code 40-1-403)
6. Oklahoma (case law)
7. Rhode Island (case law)

8. Texas (Tex. Fam. Code 2.401, 2.402)

9. Utah (Utah Code 30-1-.5)

New hampsire, also recognizes common law marriage, however only if the purpose of inheriting property from a deceased partner, and only if they lived together as a married couple for three years or until one of them dies. (N.H. Rev. Stat. 457:39 (2022). The marriage will not exist in New Hampshire until your partner dies, which allow you to claim any inheritance as a surviving spouse.

States that recognize only older common law marriages, most states recognize only common law marriages that existed before the state abolished this type of marriage. These are the States that had common law marriages that is now abolished now.

1. Alabama (befor 2017; Ala Code 30-1-20)
2. Alaska (before 1964; Alaska Stat. 25-05-061)
3. Florida (before 1968; Fla. Stat. 721.211)
4 Georgia (before 1997; Ga code 19-3-11)
5. Idaho (before 1996; Idaho code 32-201)
6. Indiana (before 1958; Ind. Code 31-11-8-5)

7. Michigan (before 1957; Mich. Com. Laws 551.2)

8. Minnesota (before 4/27/1941; Minn. Stat. 517.01)

9. Mississippi (before 4/5/1956; Miss. Code 93-15)

10. Newvada (before 3/29/1943; Nev. Rev. Stat. 122.010)

11. Ohio (before 10/10/1991; Ohio Rev. code 3105.12)

12. Phennsylvania (before 2005; 23 Pa. Cons. Stat. 1103)

13. South Carolina (before 7/ 24/ 2019; Stone V. Thompson, 833S.E.2d266 (S. C. Sup. Ct. 2019)

14. South Dokota (before 7/1/1959; S. D. Codified Laws 25-1-29), other states should recognize if you move

from a state to a state that don't have common laws, the marriage should still be valid where you live now, because Article IV of the U. S. Constitution requires State to give full faith and credit to the laws in other states including marriage laws. Ending a common law marriage, there's no such thing as common law divorce. If you had a valid common law marriage and you split up, you will need to get divorced under your state's laws, that apply to ending all marriges, that if you want the court to issue orders dividing your property or awarding alimony. If you are in a common law marriage, to change your name, you will need an official court order changing your name before you can get government agencies and many private companies, such as banks and title companies, to accept your new name. If you don't want your relationship to be a common law marriage, it would be good for you both to sign a living together agreement which is call a chobitation agreement. Waive any right to on going financial support from one another if and when you break up. This is important to have this agreement if you use the same last name, if you mix your property together or any other actions that could later be evidence to establishing a common law marriage.

CHAPTER 7

Wedding Ring

When you are grateful fear disappears and abundance appears.
Anthony Robbins

In Matthew 19:6, which says: What God has joined together, let not man put asunder. We wear the wedding ring as a beauty piece. The marriage is bounded by God and witnessed by people around us, wedding ring were popular jewelry in ancient times, before and after Christ, and if we look in the Bible it speak of several symbolic which one is symbol of favor in Luke 15:22, Genesis 41:42, Esther 3:10, Daniel 6:17. second symbol is beauty, withdrawl of favor, Jeremiah 22:24. Wedding rings in the Bible, if you look through the scriptures there is not mention of wedding bands in any verses. The rings is showing that they are making a full-time commitment to honor God in sanctity in the marriage. Therefore a circular shap wedding ring symbolizes forever marriage bonds. This ring represent eternal love of God that live in us and the love we share. As the ring is place on each other finger we are giving a symbol of love and that we are affirming the vows we have spoken to each other. As we wear these rings this will remind us of the endless circle they are. Wedding bands are perfect circle. The ring signifies there will be no end to our marriage and our happiness we will share with each other. These rings will remind us that every time we touch each other that we are sharing love and our personal lives together with Christ as the head, husband then the wife, this will show honor to each other and God favor. Marriage is not a destination however a journey, it is just a moment to moment opportunity to love and be loved the best of our ability. To get married you don't need a ring because there is no where in the Bible I have found it, so if you find it please let me know. You can always get a ring after your wedding if your heart desire. This were all initiated through man. These rings haven't kept marriages together, if so why are there so many divorces in life? We need to have true love God love the agape love: We respond calmly to each other when we are face with difficulties, sacrificing without complaining, then waiting patiently for what God have in store for us. I hope this make sense in what I am trying to explain. As I continue to write this book the ring will be explain more. To God be the Glory!!!

CHAPTER 8

WHAT DOES THE BIBLE SAY ABOUT MARRIAGE?

Great men are they who see that spirituality is stronger than any material force; that thoughts rule the world.
Ralph Waldo Emerson

The scripture teaches, husbands, love your wives (Ephesians 5:25) and teach the young women to love their husbands (Titus 2:4). In 1 Corinthians 13:4-7, this is the love that the husband should show towards his wife. In Titus 2:4, it breaks it down about teaching the younger women, verse (4 says): Paul didn't tell Titus to teach the young women. The older women had to teach them. The older women had a lot of experience and wisdom. They had learn how to be good wives and mothers, so they could advise the younger women when they had problems in married life. They could teach the younger women how to be kind to their children. When a women love someone, she does not just have good feelings. Paul describes more about the qualities of love in 1 Corinthians 13:4-8. So let's look into this scriptures: (Verse 4): People with love is patient, it is kind, it don't feel jealous, it don't boast, it is not proud. (Verse 5): It don't behave badly, It don't look out for their own interests, It don't easily become angry, It don't keep a record of how people have hurt them. (Verse 6): It take no pleasure in anything that is evil. But they are happy with the truth. (Verse7): It always protect, It always trust, It always hope, It never give up. (Verse 8): Love never come to an end. Love is permanet and without love in a marriage it is void. This is my opinion case close. This is when we have true love in our relationship or marriages once we are confident, if not confident it can make you nervous and insecure. You see each other in the future together, then you talk about it. We don't use the word me, we use the word us, when a man are in love with a woman he will view her as inseparable, he will give you more than he takes, your happiness is the reason he smile everyday, he will be with you through good and the bad, have deep sharing with each others needs. You both don't hide the truth from each other. You want to share all the good as well as the bad.

There are no other, he or she is willing to sacrifice their needs to help each other, then you know this is love. A women or a man is willing to forgive each other many times. You all push and encourage each other to be a better person, by helping each other with their dreams. You and him is there through thick and thin. You should never have to force love because it come naturally, and if it is true love it feel right with not worry, stress or doubt. When you are promise to each other this mean you both are extening your trust, and you don't play games. In true love we will be able to face challenges, losses, and failures in our life together. True love give respect for one other, as equal and we get back the same respect from one other. True love is when you can be yourself and both can accept you for who you are. True love is when you both can address your issues and solving them together. This is how we know we have real true love with someone. Just being partner to work together to solve any problems to become better in each other lives, is the fruit of true love together. True love is to be happy first with yourself then you can be happy with your partner. In love you will still have disagreements, we need not fight we need to communicate and through communication we will know what went wrong and how to solve the issues. When we are in love we will not wait to share our news with our partner whether good or bad. You can't wait to see your partner when you have been away from him all day. You will not have money issue that you both can not discuss and hide secrets. Our love for one other heals and it shows us life is beautiful and healing past hurt, toxic relationships, career failures and anything else can be heal. Everything will make sense having true love in our life. This how we can recognize red flags in a relationship before we enter in to a committed relationship.

CHAPTER 9

MARRIAGE LICENSE TRUTH

A successful marriage requires falling in love many times, always with the same person.
Mignon Mclaughlin

Marriage license truth which come out of the Black's Law Dictionary, this is my understanding, let's now proceed to enter in: When it come to marriage in the United State Of America, there are procedures and standards for marriage that one must follow, which this procedure is to acquire a marriage license.

We go about their guide line according to the state without ever knowing the reason or history and legal aspect of what they are doing. License means lacking restraint, ignoring societal standards, disregard for accepted rules. According to the Black's Law Dictionary, license means- the permission, would be illegal. This mean the government make things that was lawful to do, illegal, and which if you pay the government money (which is a bribe), then they will turn their backs and give you a permit that allows you to break the law that they say was illegal to do. So the question we need to ask ourselves, is why would it be illegal to marry without the state permission? We rarely ask or address this question because we have grown so custom, to following the laws and statutes and commadments of man, rather than the Most High. Let's go into the History of Marriage License in America and see how it came about, why it came about, and why the government and states enforce this system of enslavement upon the people.

HISTORY OF MISCEGENATION LAWS

Miscegenation laws, were laws that banned interracial marriage and sometimes interracial sex between whites and blacks. In the United States, interracial marriage, chabitation and sex have been since 1863 was us in the term as miscegenation. In North American, interracial marriage and interracial sex existed and were enforced in the thirteen colonies from the lates seventeeth century, and several US States and US Territories until; 1967. In the United State, miscegenation laws were state laws and was pass by individual states to prohibit miscegenation. Now days the word use in interracial marriage and interracial sex, which defining miscegenation as a felony, yes, felony, and these laws prohibited the solemnization of weddings between different races and prohibited officiating of such ceremonies.

BREAK DOWN OF THE SWITCH

The word fornication in the year 1303, was defined as a sexual act committed with a Prostitute. Prostitute in the Bible refers to as a harlot, which engages in sexual intercourse for money. So upon the states knowing that blacks and whites would still be tempted to marry, instead of sticking them with just felony charges, they redefined the definition of fornication, and begin using it when blacks and whites desired to marry one another, or have sex with each other, therefore making a lawful act, linked with a unlawful biblical act, bringing condemnation upon two people coming together as a sin, and illegal. So by majority states being racist states and being owners of slaves, the word fornication was instituted by scholars in to the Holy Bible, giving it's meaning or definition as sexual act when occurring outside of a marriage, any person who had sex without being married by the church. So hiding behind Christ, this racist idiotic doctrine was brought into practice, and with the new definition of of the word fornication being instituted, it gave the states a cover, to continue racism by bringing those of different races into court to be tried, for committing a felony act of fornication, thus labeling them as fornicators. Let me continue to break it down written in the Black's Law Dictionary- 5 edition: When the government need finances some states allow interracial marriges or miscegenation as long as those marrying received a license from the state. In other words they had to receive permission, and without this act such as permission would have been illegal. No long after these licenses were issued, some states began requiring all people who marry to obtain a marriage license, seeing that they could make a profit off of the union of marriage. So in 1923, the Federal Government established the uniform marriage and marriage license act (they later established the uniform marriage and divorce act). By 1929, every state in the union had adopted marriage license laws, and by 1935, all states required license except Maryland, which so followed shortly there after.

MARRIAGE LICENSES

See what we fail to realize with these procedures for marriage given by the government unto states is that, when we marrry with a marriage license, we grant the state jurisdiction over our marriages. Then your marriage become a creature of the state, it is a corporation of the state, having jurisdiction over your marriage including the fruit of your marriage, which the fruit of your marriage is your children and every piece of property you own. With a marriage license you are not just marrying your spouse, but you are also marring the state. With this ring I thee wed, is of the state and is found in most county courthouses in many states. This phrase was published by the State Bar

Association. They don't tell us when we repeat our vows, we enter into a legal contract, in which there are three parties to that contract, which the first being you, the second being the person you are marrying and the third being the state you marry in. Now the state and lawyers know when you marry with a marriage license you are not just marring your spouse, you are marrying the state, thus giving undue jurisdiction to the state. Marriage license invades and removes the Most High given parental authority. When we read the Bible, we see that the Most High intended for children to have their father's blessing regarding who they married.

Daughters were to be given in marriage by their father (Deuteronomy 22:16), (Exodus 22:17), (1 Corinthian 7:38). Why is it today when couples get married the father is suppose to be present to walk his daughter down the aisle? So man know what the word of the Most High says, so he incorporates a little in to his own agenda and personal desire to give his method of marriage some credibility. It is a known fact, there was no requirement to obtain a marriage license in Colonial America, nor in the Bible. When you read the laws of the Colonies and then the State you see only two requirements for marriage, one was you had to obtain your parents permission to marry, and second, you had to post public notice of the marriage 5-15 days before the ceremony. In the Bible the man had to obtain the father permission, abide with the father and do some work as payment for marrying his daughter, leave his father in laws house and prepare a place for his soon to be wife to live, and after a year, he would return and take unto him his wife, marriage were put on public notice in advance. You won't find nowhere in the Bible where a man ever decided to take a wife, and had to go buy a engagement ring of wedding ring, nor will you find

where a man had to acquire a
marriage license, nor will you find a
man had to go before a Preacher, or
County Clerk or Sheriff or County
judge just to be married, this Pagan
Doctrine was instituted by man, to
replace the parental right of the
father, with the philosophy of man.
Why do you think the man is sought
after for child support and spouse
support? The government knows how
to break down a man, and replace
him with welfare and child support as
being his children's father, they do as
Satan did with Eve and put the
woman over the man, therefore
crippling him not only financially, but
spiritually, by putting him in a

position as the weaker vessel and subject to the authority of his wife, that's totally against the order of the Most High. Most preachers who are under seminary delusion, have no idea that when they are marrying someone with a marriage license, they are acting as a agent of the State rather than a man of the Most High. Some Peachers of the Most High, is committing treason against the Most High, by acting as an agent by representing the laws and commandments of the State. A marriage license is a three-party contract between the man, woman, and the State known as a adhesion contract. An adhesion contract is one which is extremly one-sided, grossly favoring the State. When you apply for a marriage license, your are asking for permission to engage in the unlawful activity of marriage. (Black's Law 7th ed). Why? Because the State can regulate that which it licenses, by entering into a State-Sanctioned Franchise (marriage) as a married couple, a couple forfeits the rights to a private, sovereign marriage and any ownership control of their children or property; as a result of the marriage license. Child Protective Service receives their full power and authority to seize children via the marriage license under the ancient legal doctrine parens patriae.

When a state licensed married couple
have a child, the Birth Certificate is
the document of the state uses to
claim ownership of the child under it
marriage contract. State ownership
remains as long as the child lives,
even after the age of 21. If we have a
birth certificate, the state own us
too. Couples married under a state-
sanctioned marriage license also give
up 1/3 of their property to the State.
Should one person die, the
government through the inheritance
tax, will demand the suviving party to
buy them out-usually a 28-35% tax.
Amost all Peachers who marry a
couple who has marriage licenses,
marry them by the authority vested in

them by the State, not by the Most High as they loudly and lyingly proclaim. A certificate in Barron's Banking Dictionary defines a certificate as a paper establishing an ownership claim. In 1903 only a few states had adopted a marriage license scheme, yes scheme because that is what it is used for today. Birth Certificates, Marriage Certificates and Automobile Certificates of title are just some of the commerical paper the State Government use to collateralize their debt to the banks for all of the bond issues the people vote for. These certificates are serial numbered so the banks can more easily track them and all conform to the rules of negotiable instruments as out lined in the uniform commercial code. You and your family have in effect, been pledged as chattel to the banks for the State's and Federal Government's Debts.

MARRIAGE LIENSE- THE INSITITUTION OF (CHILD PROTECTIVE SERVICES)

America never had a child protective services protecting our children for at least the first 140 years, because assault on a child was already illegal and dealt with by the County Sheriff. If a child needed to be removed to a safer and private place. This competition forced the homes to maintain extremely high standards and, due to the limitation of funds, resolving family problems and reuniting the child with his family was the primary importance- unlike today's Stat-Administered System of bureaucratic red tape, and drugging programs that will damage a child for the rest of his or her life and ultimately alienate him from his family. This is the conclusion on marriage license, let look at the phrase the Government uses, In God We Trust, which is a lie, because the Government is against everything the Most High stands for. Our trust should be in the Most High, Laws, Statutes and Commandments. When the standard and procedures of the United States Of America are not in compliance with the Most High, as followers of the Most High this is what to do: Acts 5:29. FYI: You should want to obey the Most High rather than the Government! So when it come down to marriage in the United States of America, which is commanded by the government those intending to be married, must have a marriage license, so if you believe and following the Most High, then we should not yield ourselves servant to the Government unrighteousness. Case Close, I have given you (us) what the Black's Law Dictionary has said. (The 5, 7 ed.) I don't know much, however this is what I found, when I ask the question after my last divorce and this is the answer I got. This is when I got the truth. We all have been lead wrong and some of us don't want to come out of the old tradition by man. 2 Corinthians 5:17: Therefore if any man be in Christ, he is a new creature; old things are passed away; behold, all things are become new.

CHAPTER 10

BINDING OF HANDS, (GROOM) AND (BRIDE)

A perfect marriage is just two imperfect people who refuse to give up on each other.
Kate Stewart

Three cord strands ceremony meaning in Ecclesiastes 4: 12, in the Bible it tell us that through one strand of cord we can be overpowered, which two can defend each other and a cord strand three can not be easily broken in a marriage. These cord represent God, the groom and the bride and when the cords are join together it symbolize one man, one woman and God in our marriage. When we keep God in the center of our marriage his love will continue to make the marriage strong, grow and to stay together. This happen toward the end of the ceremony. This is how it is done, the groom holds the top ring connecting the cord, and bride braids the strands together, this symbolize the union between husband, wife and God. After the unity braid is done, the officiant or whoever wraps the couple's hands with it by draping the braid over their shoulder to show the bond between the both of them.

This is what the cord of the strands represent: which is the element of their bond. Which the color Gold Strand represent God, is to glorify him and building of his covenant in the relationship. The Color Strand Purple represent the groom and the White represent the bride. You can customize your cord to any color to match your wedding scheme. This is what is said when binding of hands: (Goom) and (Bride), I bind as you look in each other eyes, will you honor and respect one another, and seek to never break that honor? We will (the first cord is draped over the couples hands) and so the first binding is made. Will you share each other's pain and seek to ease it? We will (second cord is draped over the hand and so the binding is made. Will you share the intention of each, so that your spirits may grow in this union? We will (Third cord is draped over the couples hands). Now the binding is made. Will you share each other's laughter, and look for the brightness in life and the positive in each other? We will (fourth cord is draped over the couples hands) so there are two ways you can do this. I hope this make sense to you'll. These are just some ideas that you may want to incorporate in your wedding. All I can say is keep it simple and short in the eye of God (The Most High)!!!

CHAPTER 11

FIVE REASON WHY WE SHOULDN'T OBTAIN A STATE MARRIAGE LICENSES

Marriage is not some fairytale, It is love Selflessness, Patience, Tolerance and Enduring the Hard Time Together.
Unknown

1. It is Illegal, Why should we need the State Permission to participate in something which God instituted (Genesis 2:18-24). The State cannot grant the right to marry, It is a God given right.

2. When you marry with a marriage license you grant the State Jurisdiction over your marriage. In 1993, Parents were upset in Wisconsin because a test was being administered to their children in the Government Schools which was very invasive of the family's privacy. When the Parents complained, they were shocked by the school bureaucrates who informed them that their children were required to take the test by law and that they would have to take the test because they (the Government School) had jurisdiction over their children. The question by parents was what gave them the right? They answered, your marriage license and

their birth certificates.

3. By obtaining a marriage license, you place yourself under jurisdiction of family court which is governed by unbibilcal and immoral laws. Under these laws, you can divorce for any reason. Any pastor who marry someone with marriage license they are acting as an agent of the State.

4. The married license invades and remove God-given parental authority. When you read the Bible you see that God intended for children to have their father's blessings regarding whom they married. Daughters were to be given in marriage by their

fathers, (Deuteronomy 22:16, Exodus 22:17, 1 Corinthians 7:38). Historically, there was no requirement to obtain a marriage license in Colonia America. When you read the laws of the Colonies and then the States, there were only two requirements for marriage: First you had to obtain your parents permission to marry, and second you had to post public notice of the marriage 5-15 days before the ceremony. By issuing marriage licenses, the State is saying, you don't need your parents permission. This is an invasion and removal of God-given parental authority by the State.

5. From the State's point of view, when you marry with a marriage license you are not just marrying your spouse, but you are also marrying the State. I have some of the same things in Chapter Nine Marriage License Truth. God intended the State to have Jurisdiction over a marriage for two reason: 1. In case of divorce. 2. When crimes are committed, adultery, bigamy, ect.

What is needed in a marriage are witnesses. This is why you would want a best man and a maid of honor. They should sign the marriage certificate in your Family Bible, and the wedding day guest book should be kept. Marriage was instituted by God, therefore it is a God-given right. According to scripture, it is to be governed by the Family, and the State only!!! have jurisdiction in cases of divorce or crime. History of marriage license in America, look at George Washington he was married without a marriage license. This started in 1800 with certain states began allowing interracial marriages or miscegenation as long as they receive a license from the State. When you want to be married without a license: Get a Family Bible that have in it Birth, Death records and a Marriage Certificate. Record the marriage in the Family Bible.

What is recorded in a Family Bible will stand up as legal evidence in any court of law in America. Early Americans were married without a married license. They simply recorded their marriages in their Family Bible, so should we. For those who don't believe go with the Government. Everyone have their own beliefs, all I can say and my opinion is to follow the spirit that live inside of you. My beliefs and my opinion is not yours. I am just giving some sound advice. Some of us love a lie more than the truth. Romans 3:4, God tell the truth, even if everyone else is a liar. The scripture say about God, your words will be proven true, and in court you will win your case. Some of us might know already about the truth about why we shouldn't obtain a State License, however we close our eyes to the truth and sweep it under the rug. Be continually bless as our mind and heart is open to the truth.

CHAPTER 12

WHAT TITUS HAD TO TEACH

Marriage is about finding someone who knows you are not perfect, but treats you as if you are.
Marriage Quotes

We must follow the spirit and not our flesh, the spirit lead to life and the flesh lead to destruction.(Romans 8:6) take time to read this scripture for yourself. So let me move on to Titus in what he is teaching us about what we should be doing to teach the younger generation.

I was told by a close friend that is no longer in this life to tell all men to read the Book of Titus, he didn't tell me the reason, just know Titus only have three chapters, it's short and sweet. I was told by another sister that is not in this life, she said to eat it all, it was going to be bitter when it go down inside of me, but it will be sweet when it come back up. What she was saying everything I read was not going to be sweet, but after I digested, I would be able to absorbe it better and it would become sweet coming out as I explain it to others. So I am going into Titus Chapter 2.

This what Titus had to teach as we should do also. He is teaching us how some time we are taught many wrong things. He had to teach what was true and we have to do the same We have to teach others how to behave in the right way that the spirit is leading us to do. In Verse 2, It is telling us about older men: what they should do, which say they should be mature, not behave in foolish ways. We already know younger people will copy from us, so we should be good role models. Older men should not drink too much wine, because they will not be able to think clearly. They should be older men, someone the young can respect, should be serious and not be silly, because life will come to an end. Must be able to control their words and actions. Must trust God completely as they believe the true gospel message. As they trust God they will love him more, they should be able to understand people more. Sometime being older we tend to complain about people more. They should be patient, have courage when life is difficult. Now let go to verse 3, It talks about the older women: Older women should behave in a mature way too. Should always try to please God. We have more spare time because our children are adults. In society women often met together to gossip about other people and drink too much wine.

To speak badly mean to say evil things and to lie. We should be good role models for othe people to copy. Using our time wisely. We should be teaching in our homes, speaking about good things. Verse 4, Titus was not to teach the young women. The older women had to teach them. We are the one who have a lot of experience and wisdom. Older women had learn how to be good wives and mothers. This is why we have to advise the younger women when they had problems in married life. We can teach the younger women how to be kind to their children. When we love someone, we don't just have good feelings. There are more about the qualities of love in 1 Corinthians 13: 3-4. Verse 5, Talk about the young women: Some young women were married, some were widows. Paul suggested that widows should marry again (1 Timothy 5:14-15). 1. Young women should learn how to control themselves. Should be sensible, and should behave well 2. Should be pure. Avoid sin, having a good character, and morally good. 3. Married women should work in their home, and to be responsible for everything that happened in her home. Should not be lazy and should be willing to work hard, also serve her husband and her family. 4. should be kind, when you're kind she is helpful, she tries to please other people, so she is not selfish. 5. Should obey their husband, and she know he is the head in their home. Ephesians 5:22-24. It is easy for a wife to obey her husband if she loves him, she should respect him too. When women behave in these ways, then no one can say evil things about them. This is also about wives, husbands that might not believe, however if wives made a safe and happy home the husband will believe the good news if their wives obey them. (1 Peter 3:1-2). Then the good news would attract other people. Verse 6, Talk about young men: Paul use the strong word urge: This mean to teach and to persuade. Sometime young men are often tempted to do

wrong things. Sometime they can be too confident because they don't have enough experience or wisdom. They may live or work away from the discipline of a good home. Maybe careless about friends that they choose. If not married, they can please themselves. If they have a wife and family, they may not relise their responsibilities. Young men should control: 1. How they act
2. What they say
3. What they think about
4. How they express their emotions
5. Their desires

Verse 7, Paul told Titus and Timothy to be a good model.

1 Timothy 4:12. Titus had to be a model in evey way. He had to teach the truth and behave in the right way. This would show he taught the truth. The false teachers said that they taught the truth, however they behaved in a bad way. Being honest mean to be sincere. Titus had to show his intetion was good, and had to teach for the right reason. (The false teachers taught for financial profit, 1:11) He had to be serious, Titus as a teacher had an important job, by being aware of his responsibility. Verse 8, Titus had to be careful about everything he said in public or private conversation. He had to be sensible,

and always had to speak the truth. People watch Titus and listened to him. They were ready to accuse him, however Titus could show that they were wrong. Now people would see Titus was different from false teachers, and as a result, some of them would believe the good news about Jesus. Now we as seasonal adults know what we should be teaching our young men and women on how to be good wives and mother's to their family's. No one want to peach or teach about this subject because we are trying to be their friends and not Elders to the young to help send the next generation in the right direction. There may be someone that don't want to hear and there are some who might want to hear this. This is why in Matthew 7:6, tell us don't give that which is Holy to the pigs be cause they are not ready for it. They can not see the difference between what is valuable and what is not valuable. This is not to be force it's free will, however there blood are on our hands, if we know the truth and don't tell it to those God (Our Most High) have put us over. Sometime we are not going to reach everyone because they are not ready and everyone is not where we are in our journey in life. When we are teaching and someone is not ready, we have to move on to those who are ready.

BONUS 1

WHEN SOMETHING GOES WRONG

1. TOO SALTY – Soup and stew, add cut raw potatoes and discard once they have cooked and absorbed the salt. You can do something else, you can add a teaspoon each of cider vinegar and sugar or simply add sugar.

IF SOMETHING TOO SWEET

2. Add salt, if it's a main dish or vegetable, add a teaspoon of cider vinegar.

BONUS 2

KEEPING FOOD FRESH

Bacon and Sauage- To prevent bacon from curling, dip the strips in cold water before frying.
Bacon will lie flat in the pan if you pick it thoroughly with a fork as it fries.
Keep bacon slices from sticking together; roll the package into a tube shape and secure with rubber bands.
A quick way to separate frozen bacon bacon: Heat a spatula over the stove burner, then slide it under each slice to separate it from the others.
Have you ever tried to get roll sausage out of a package, only to find that

half of it is stuck to the surrounding paper? Try running cold water over the paper before you remove the contents. Or, let it set in cold ice water for awhile.

BANANAS- Toss freshly peeled banana in lemon juice and they will not darken.

Freeze bananas that are on the verge of going bad they also make delicious popsicles.

If they've darkened peel and beat slightly. Put into a plastic container and freeze until it's time to bake bread or cake.

BONUS 3

THE CAR

Washing your car- In stead of washing your car with soap and water, try washing with a bucker of water and 1 cup kerosene followed by a good wiping with soft cloths. The best part of it is that no matter how dirty your car is it will not need wetting down before starting, nor rinsing once you have finished. When it rains the car will actually bead off water. It helps prevent rust. Use no wax with this method.

Quick cleaning windows- Baking soda

quickly cleans spatters and traffic grime from windshields, headlights, chrome and enamel. Wipe with soda sprinkled onto a damp sponge. Rinse. Use plastic net bags (the kind onions come in) to wash windshields when insects have accumulated. Simply tie a few bags into one bag and rub away.

PREVENTING DOORS AND TRUNK FROM FREEZING

Wipe or spray the rubber gaskets with a heavy coating of vegetable oil. The oil will seal out water, but will not harm the gasket. This is easpecially good before having your car washed in the winter.

WRITE NOTES:

WRITE NOTES:

WRITE NOTES:

WRITE NOTES:

NOTES